A Tomb for Anatole

by Stéphane Mallarmé

Translated and with an Introduction
by Paul Auster

•

NORTH POINT PRESS
San Francisco
1983

Grateful acknowledgment is made to *The Paris Review* and
Pequod, in which portions of this work previously appeared.

Mallarmé's second child, Anatole, was born on July 16, 1871, when the poet was twenty-nine. The boy's arrival came at a moment of great financial stress and upheaval for the family. Mallarmé was in the process of negotiating a move from Avignon to Paris, and arrangements were not finally settled until late November, when the family installed itself at 29 rue de Moscou and Mallarmé began teaching at the Lycée Fontanes.

Mme Mallarmé's pregnancy had been extremely difficult, and in the first months of his life Anatole's health was so fragile that it seemed unlikely he would survive. "I took him out for a walk on Thursday," Mme Mallarmé wrote to her husband on October 7. "It seemed to me that his fine little face was getting back some of its color. . . . I left him very sad and discouraged, and even afraid that I would not see him anymore, but it's up to God now, since the doctor can't do anything more, but how sad to have so little hope of seeing this dear little person recover."

Anatole's health, however, did improve. Two years later, in 1873, he reappears in the family correspondence in a series of letters from Germany, where Mallarmé's wife had taken the children to meet her father. "The little one is like a blossoming flower," she wrote to Mallarmé. "Tole loves his grandfather, he does not want to leave him, and when he is gone, he looks for him all over the house." In that same letter, nine-year-old Geneviève added: "Anatole asks for papa all the time." Two years later, on a second trip to Germany, there is further evidence of Anatole's robust health, for after receiving a letter from his wife, Mallarmé wrote proudly to his friend Cladel: "Anatole showers stones and punches on the little Germans who come back to attack him in a group." The following year, 1876, Mallarmé was absent from Paris for a few days and received this anecdote from his wife: "Totol is a bad little boy. He did not notice you were gone the night you left; it was only when I put him to bed that he looked everywhere for you to say good-night. Yesterday he did not ask for you, but this morning the poor little fellow looked all over the house for you; he even pulled back the covers on your bed, thinking he would find you there." In August of that same year, during another of Mallarmé's brief absences from the family, Geneviève wrote to her father to thank him for sending her presents and then remarked: "Tole wants you to bring him back a whale."

Beyond these few references to Anatole in the Mallarmé family letters, there are several mentions of him in C. L. Lefèvre-Roujon's introduction to the *Correspondance inédite de Stéphane Mallarmé et Henry Roujon*—in particular, three little incidents that give some idea of the boy's lively personality. In the first, a stranger saw Anatole attending to his father's boat and asked him, "What is your boat called?" Anatole answered with great conviction, "My boat isn't called anything. Do you give a name to a carriage?" On another occasion, Anatole was taking a walk through the Fountainebleau forest with Mallarmé. "He loved the Fountainebleau forest and would often go there with Stéphane. . . . [One day], running down a path, he came upon a very pretty woman, politely stepped to the side, looked her over from top to bottom and, out of admiration, winked his eye at her, clicked his tongue, and then, this homage to beauty having been made, continued on his child's promenade." Finally, Lefèvre-Roujon reports the following: One day Mme Mallarmé boarded a Paris bus with Anatole and put the child on her lap in order to economize on the extra fare. As the bus jolted along, Anatole fell into a kind of trance, watching a gray-haired priest beside him who was reading his breviary. He asked him sweetly: "Monsieur l'abbée, would you allow me to kiss you?" The priest, surprised and touched, answered: "But of course, my little friend." Anatole leaned over and kissed him. Then, in the suavest voice possible, he commanded: "And now, kiss mama!"

In the spring of 1879, several months before his eighth birthday, Anatole became seriously ill. The disease, diagnosed as child's rheumatism, was further complicated by an enlarged heart. The illness first attacked his feet and knees, and then, when the symptoms had apparently cleared up, his ankles, wrists, and shoulders. Mallarmé considered himself largely responsible for the child's suffering, feeling that he had given the boy "bad blood" through a hereditary weakness. At the age of seventeen, he had suffered terribly from rheumatic pain, with high fevers and violent headaches, and throughout his life rheumatism would remain a chronic problem.

In April, Mallarmé went off to the country for a few days with

Geneviève. His wife wrote: "He's been a good boy, the poor little martyr, and from time to time asks me to dry his tears. He asks me often to tell little papa that he would like to write to him, but he can't move his little wrists." Three days later, the pain had shifted from Anatole's hands to his legs, and he was able to write a few words: "I think of you always. If you knew, my dear Little Father, how my knees hurt."

Over the following months, things took a turn for the better. By August, the improvement had been considerable. On the tenth, Mallarmé wrote to Robert de Montesquiou, a recently made friend who had formed a special attachment to Anatole, to thank him for sending the child a parrot. "I believe that your delicious little animal . . . has distracted the illness of our patient, who is now allowed to go to the country. . . . Have you heard from where you are . . . all the cries of joy from our invalid, who never takes his eyes . . . away from the marvelous princess held captive in her marvelous palace, who is called Sémiramas because of the stone gardens she seems to reflect? I like to think that this satisfaction of an old and improbable desire has had something to do with the struggle of the boy's health to come back; to say nothing . . . of the secret influence of the precious stone that darts out continually from the cage's inhabitant on the child. . . . How charming and friendly you have been, you who are so busy with so much, during this recent time; and it is more than a pleasure for me to announce to you, before anyone else, that I feel all our worries will soon be over."

In this state of optimism, Anatole was taken by the family to Valvins in the country. After several days, however, his condition deteriorated drastically, and he nearly died. On August 22, Mallarmé wrote to his close friend Henry Roujon:

"I hardly dare to give any news because there are moments in this war between life and death that our poor little adored one is waging when I allow myself to hope, and repent of a too sad letter written the moment before, as of some messenger of bad tidings I myself have dispatched. I know nothing anymore and see nothing anymore . . . so much have I observed with conflicting emotions. The doctor, while continuing the Paris treatment, seems to act as though he were dealing with a condemned person who can only be comforted; and persists, when I follow him to the door, in not giving a glimmer of hope. The dear boy eats and sleeps a little; breathes. Everything his organs could do to fight the heart problem they have done; after another enormous attack, that is the benefit he draws from the country. But the disease, the terrible disease, seems to have set in irremediably. If you lift the blanket, you see a belly so swollen you can't look at it!

"There it is. I do not speak to you of my pain; no matter where my thought tries to lead it, this pain recoils from seeing itself worsen! But what does suffering matter, even suffering like that: the horrible thing is . . . the misfortune in itself that this little being might vanish. . . . I confess that it is too much for me; I cannot bring myself to face this idea.

"When my wife looks at the darling, she seems to see a serious illness and nothing more; I must not rob her of the courage she has found to care for the child in this quietude. I am alone here then with the hatchet blow of the doctor's verdict."

A letter from Mallarmé to Montesquiou on September 9 offers further details: "Unfortunately, after several days [in the country], everything . . . grew dark: we have been through the cruelest hours our darling invalid has caused us, for the symptoms we thought had disappeared forever have returned; they are taking hold now. The old improvements were a sham. . . . I am too tormented and too taken up with our poor little boy to do anything literary, except to jot down a few rapid notes. . . . *Tole* speaks of you, and even amuses himself in the morning by fondly imitating your voice. The parrot, whose auroral belly seems to catch fire with a whole orient of spices, is looking right now at the forest with one eye and at the bed with the other, like a thwarted desire for an excursion by her little master."

By late September there had been no improvement, and Mallarmé now centered his hopes on a return to Paris. On the twenty-fifth, he wrote to his oldest friend, Henri Cazalis: "The evening before your beautiful present came, the poor darling, for the second time since his illness began, was nearly taken from us. Three successive fainting fits in the afternoon did not, thank heaven, carry him off. . . . The belly disturbs us, as filled with water as ever. . . . The country has given us everything we could ask of it, assuming it could give us anything, milk, air, and peaceful surroundings for the invalid. We have only one idea now, to leave for a consultation with

Doctor Peter. . . . I tell myself it is impossible that a great medical specialist cannot take advantage of the forces nature opposes so generously to a terrible disease. . . ."

After the return to Paris, there are two further letters about Anatole—both dated October 6. The first was to the English writer John Payne: "This is the reason for my long silence. . . . At Easter, already six hideous months ago, my son was attacked by rheumatism, which after a false convalescence has thrown itself on his poor heart with incredible violence, and holds him between life and death. The poor friend has twice almost been taken from us. . . . You can judge of our pain, knowing how much I live inside my family; then this child, so charming and exquisite, had captivated me to the point that I still include him in all my future projects and in my dearest dreams. . . ."

The other letter was to Montesquiou. "Thanks to immense precautions, everything went well [on the return to Paris] . . . but the darling paid for it with several bad days that drained his tiny energy. He is prey to a horrible and inexplicable nervous cough. . . . it shakes him for a whole day and a whole night. . . . —Yes, I am quite beside myself, like someone on whom a terrible and endless wind is blowing. All-night vigils, contradictory emotions of hope and sudden fear, have supplanted all thought of repose. . . . My sick little boy smiles at you from his bed, like a white flower remembering the vanished sun."

After writing these two letters, Mallarmé went to the post office to mail them. Anatole died before his father managed to return home.

•

The 202 fragments that follow belonged to Mme E. Bonniot, the Mallarmé heir, and were deciphered, edited, and published in a scrupulously prepared volume by the literary scholar and critic Jean-Pierre Richard in 1961. In the preface to his book—which includes a lengthy study of the fragments—he describes his feelings on being handed the soft red box that contained Mallarmé's notes. On the one hand: exaltation. On the other hand: wariness. Although he was deeply moved by the fragments, he was uncertain whether publication was appropriate, given the intensely private nature of the work. He concluded, however, that anything that could enhance our understanding of Mallarmé would be valuable. "And if these phrases are no more than sighs," he wrote, "that makes them all the more precious to us. It seemed to me that the very nakedness of these notes . . . made their distribution desirable. It was useful in fact to prove once again to what extent the famous Mallarméan serenity was based on the impulses of a very vivid sensibility, at times even quite close to frenzy and delirium. . . . Nor was it irrelevant to show, by means of a precise example, how this impersonality, this vaunted objectivity, was in reality connected to the most subjective upheavals of a life."

A close reading of the fragments will clearly show that they are no more than notes for a possible work: a long poem in four parts with a series of very specific themes. That Mallarmé projected such a work and then abandoned it is indicated in a memoir written by Geneviève that was published in a 1926 issue of the N.R.F.: "In 1879, we had the immense sorrow of losing my little brother, an exquisite child of eight. I was quite young then, but the deep and silent pain I felt in my father made an unforgettable impression on me: 'Hugo,' he said, 'was happy to have been able to speak (about the death of his daughter); for me, it's impossible.' "

As they stand now, the notes are a kind of ur-text, the raw data of the poetic process. Although they seem to resemble poems on the page, they should not be confused with poetry per se. Nevertheless, more than one hundred years after they were written, they are perhaps closer to what we today consider possible in poetry than at the time of their composition. For here we find a language of immediate contact, a syntax of abrupt, lightning shifts that still manages to maintain a sense, and in their brevity, the sparse presence of their words, we are given a rare and early example of isolate words able to span the enormous mental spaces that lie between them—as if intelligible links could be created by the brute force of each word or phrase, so densely charged that these tiny particles of language could somehow leap out of themselves and catch hold of the succeeding cliff-edge of thought. Unlike Mallarmé's finished poems, these fragments have a startlingly unmediated quality. Faithful not to the demands of art but to the jostling movement of thought—and with a speed and precision that astonish—these notes seem to emerge from such an interior place, it is as though we could hear the crackling of the wires in Mallarmé's brain, experience each synapse of thought as a physical sensation. If these fragments cannot be read as a work of art, neither, I think, should they be treated simply as a scholarly appendage to Mallarmé's collected writings. For, in spite of everything, the Anatole notes do carry the force of poetry, and in the end they achieve a stunning wholeness. They are a work in their own right—but one that cannot be categorized, one that does not fit into any preexistant literary form.

The subject matter of the fragments requires little comment. In general, Mallarmé's motivation seems to have been the following: feeling himself responsible for the disease that led to Anatole's death, for not giving his son a body strong enough to withstand the blows of life, he would take it upon himself to give the boy the one indomitable thing he was capable of giving: his thought. He would transmute Anatole into words and thereby prolong his life. He would, *literally*, resurrect him, since the work of building a tomb— a tomb of poetry—would obliterate the presence of death. For Mallarmé, death is the consciousness of death, not the physical act of dying. Because Anatole was too young to understand his fate (a theme that occurs repeatedly throughout the fragments), it was as though he had not yet died. He was still alive in his father, and it was only when Mallarmé himself died that the boy would die as well. This is one of the most moving accounts of a man trying to come to grips with modern death—that is to say, death without God, death without hope of salvation—and it reveals the secret meaning of Mallarmé's entire aesthetic: the elevation of art to the stature of religion. Here, however, the work could not be written. In this time of crisis even art failed Mallarmé.

It strikes me that the effect of the Anatole fragments is quite close to the feeling created by Rembrandt's last portrait of his son, Titus. Bearing in mind the radiant and adoring series of canvasses the artist made of the boy throughout his childhood, it is almost impossible for us to look at that last painting: the dying Titus, barely twenty years old, his face so ravaged by disease that he looks like an old man. It is important to imagine what Rembrandt must have felt as he painted that portrait; to imagine him staring into the face of his dying son and being able to keep his hand steady enough to put what he saw onto the canvas. If fully imagined, the act becomes almost unthinkable.

In the natural order of things, fathers do not bury their sons. The death of a child is the ultimate horror of every parent, an outrage against all we believe we can expect of life, little though it is. For everything, at that point, is taken away from us. Unlike Ben Jonson, who could lament the fact of his fatherhood as an impediment to understanding that his son had reached "the state he should envie," Mallarmé could find no support for himself, only an abyss, no consolation, except in the plan to write about his son—which, in the end, he could not bring himself to do. The work died along with Anatole. It is all the more moving to us, all the more important, for having been left unfinished.

•

In working on this translation over a number of years, I have been helped by several friends, and I have hoarded this moment to give them my thanks: Claude Royet-Journoud, for introducing the book to me in 1971; Mary Ann Caws, for reviving the project through her edition of Mallarmé's selected writings with New Directions; Jonathan Galassi, for his painstaking work with me in making a selection of the fragments for the *Paris Review*; and Michael Palmer, for his constant encouragement and astute reading of the final manuscript. Mention should also be made of Jean-Pierre Richard's excellent edition of the French text. His thorough introduction has provided me with the biographical information about Anatole as well as the excerpts from the Mallarmé family letters, and his study of the fragments has been an important tool in my efforts to crack the obscure and difficult passages that appear throughout the work. Finally, I have borrowed and slightly modified the title he has given the notes, *Pour un tombeau d'Anatole*, which I find appropriate in all its ramifications.

P.A.
New York; Oct. 6, 1982

A Tomb for Anatole

child sprung from
the two of us — showing
us our ideal, the way
— ours! father
and mother who
        sadly existing
survive him as
the two extremes —
badly coupled in him
and sundered
— from whence his death — o-
bliterating this little child "self"

1

•

enfant sorti de
nous deux — nous
montrant notre
idéal, le chemin
— à nous! père
et mère qui lui
        en triste existence
survivons comme
les deux extrêmes —
mal associés en lui
et qui se sont séparés
— d'où sa mort — annu-
lant ce petit «soi» d'enfant

2

better
as if he ⟨when⟩
still were —
whatever they may have been,
of epithets
worthy — etc.
the hours when
you were and
were not

•

⟨3
meilleures
comme s'il ⟨quand⟩
était encore —
quelqu'ils fussent,
des qualificatifs
digne — etc.
les heures où
vous fûtes et ne
fûtes pas

sick in
        springtime
dead in fall
        — it is the sun
                ———

        the wave
idea   the cough
2

•

malade au
        printemps
mort en automne
        — c'est le soleil
                ———

        la vague
idée   la toux
2

4

son
 reabsorbed
not gone
 it is he
— or his brother
 myself
 I told this
 to him
 two brothers
 —

•

fils
 résorbé
pas parti
 c'est lui
— ou son frère
 moi
 je le lui
 ai dit
 deux frères
 —

forced back remaining
in the womb —
⟨only⟩ upon myself
      century
will not flow out
only
     to instruct me.

5

•

refoulée restée
en flanc —
⟨juste⟩ sur de moi
      siècle
ne s'écoulera pas
juste pour
     m'instruire.

6

did not know
mother, and son did
not know me! —
— image of myself
other than myself
borne off
in death!

•

pas connu
mère, et fils ne
m'a pas connu! —
— image de moi
autre que moi
emporté en
mort!

what has taken refuge
your future   in me
          becomes my
purity through life,
which I shall not
     touch —

·

          qui s'est réfugié
ton futur   en moi
          devient ma
pureté à travers vie,
à laquelle je ne
     toucherai pas —

8

it is   era of
      one
the Existence in which we
find ourselves,
    if not a place —
— and if you
      doubt it
      the world will
      be the witness,
assuming that
  I live to be that old

———

•

il est   époque de
      une
l'Existence où nous
  nous retrouverons,
    sinon un lieu —
— et si vous
      en doutez
      le monde en
      sera témoin,
en supposant que
  je vive assez vieux

———

father who
  born in a bad
time had
  prepared for son —
  a sublime task

—

"the double one to
be filled — the child's
his own — the pain the desire
to sacrifice himself to one who is
no more will triumph over
strength (the man he did not become)
and who will carry out the child's task

•

père qui
  né en temps
mauvais avait
  préparé à fils —
  une tâche sublime

—

«la double à
remplir — d'enfant
la sienne — la douleur le désir
de se sacrifier à qui n'est
plus l'emporteront-ils sur
vigueur (homme qu'il n'a pas été)
et fera-t-il la tâche de l'enfant

10

the supreme goal
was nothing
but to leave life
purely
    you did this
in advance
  by suffering
    so much — sweet
    child so that
It will count against
your lost life — your family
has bought the rest by their
        suffering from having you
            no longer

•

le but suprême
n'eût été
que partir pur
de la vie
    tu l'as accompli
d'avance
  en souffrant
    assez — doux
    enfant pour que
Cela te soit compté
pour ta vie perdue — les tiens
ont acheté le reste par leur
        souffrance de ne plus t'avoir

to pray to the dead
(not for them)

—

    knees, child
    knees — need
to have the child here
    — his absence — knees
fall — and

———

for one of the true dead
only a child!

•

prier morts
(non pour eux)

—

    genoux, enfant
    genoux — besoin
d'y avoir l'enfant
    — son absence — genoux
tombent — et

———

car de vrais morts
qu'enfant!

12

(2

hands join
towards the one who can
not be touched —
but who is —
— that a space
divides —

•

(2

mains se joignent
vers celui qu'on
ne peut presser —
mais qui est —
— qu'un espace
sépare —

dear one

— great heart
⟨tr⟩ truly son of ⟨who⟩
            father whose
heart
beat for things
    too vast
    — and which came here
    to fail
        it was necessary —
inheriting this
marvelous fil-
ial intelligence, making

•

chéri

— grand cœur
⟨bi⟩ bien fils de ⟨qui⟩
            père dont
le cœur
battit pour projets
    trop grands
    — et venus là
    échouer
        il fallait —
héritant de cette
merveilleuse intelli-
gence filiale, la

14

(2

it live again
— to construct
with his ⟨clear⟩
lucidity — this
work — too
    vast for me

and thus, (robbing
me of
life, sacri-
ficing it, if it

•

(2

faisant revivre
— construire
avec sa ⟨nette⟩
lucidité — cette
œuvre — trop
    vaste pour moi

et ainsi, (me
privant de la
vie, la sacri-
fiant, si ce

(3

is not for the wk
— to be him grown up,
⟨robbed⟩ of — and
to do this without
fear of <u>playing</u>
with his death —
since I
sacrificed my
life to him — since
I accepted as
my own this death
(cloistering)

•

(3

n'est pour l'œ
— être lui grand,
⟨privé⟩ de — et
faire cela sans
crainte de <u>jouer</u>
avec sa mort —
puisque je lui
sacrifiais ma
vie — puisque
j'acceptais quant à
moi cette mort
(claustration)

16

example
    we have known
through you this "better
part of ourselves"
which often
escapes us — and will be
within us — and our
acts, now

————

child, planting
    idealization

•

exemple
    nous avons su
par toi ce «meilleur
de nous-mêmes»
qui souvent nous
échappe — et sera
en nous — en nos
actes, maintenant

————

enfant, semence
    idéalisation

father and mother
 vowing
 to have no other
child
    — grave dug by him
    life ends here

•

père et mère se
 promettant de
 n'avoir pas d'autre
enfant
    — fosse creusée par lui
    vie cesse là

18

vain
   cures
      abandoned
if nature
did not will it

—

   I would take
   myself for
   dead

balms, only,
consolations for us
  — doubt
then no! their reality

•

   remèdes
     vains
       laissés
  si nature
  n'a pas voulu

  —

    j'en trouverai
    moi pour
    mort

baumes, seulement,
consolations pour nous
  — doute
puis non! leur réalité

child our
immortality
 in fact made
of buried human
hopes — son —
confided to the wife
by the man de-
spairing after youth
to find the mystery
and taking a wife

———

•

enfant notre
immortalité
 en effet fait
d'espoirs humains
enfouis — fils —
confiés à la femme
par l'homme déses-
pérant après jeunesse
de trouver le mystère
et prenant femme

———

20

sick
   since the day when death
moved in — marked by
sickness —
already is no longer himself, but
is the one through
death we would later
want to see again —
summing up death and
corruption — appearing
like that, with his sickness
   and his pallor

•

malade
   depuis le jour où mort
s'installe — marqué par
maladie —
n'est plus lui déjà, mais
est celui qu'à travers
la mort plus tard on
voudrait revoir —
résumant mort et
corruption — apparu
tel, avec son mal
   et sa pâleur

(2

⌈sick — to be naked
⌊like the child —

and appearing before us
— we take advantage of these
hours, when death
                struck down
he lives
            again, and
    again is ours

title poetry of
            the sickness.

•

                    (2
⌈malade — être à nu
⌊comme l'enfant —

et nous apparaissant
— l'on profite de ces
heures, où mort
                    frappé
il vit
            encore, et
    est encore à nous

titre poésie de
            la maladie.

22

with gift of word
I could have made you
    you,   the child of the wk.
  king made of you
      instead
— no, sad   of the son
      in us
  — made you — of
      task
    no —
      no he
remember the proves
      he was
bad days — that —
      played
mouth shut, etc. this role!
    natal
— etc. word —
      forgotten
it is I who
have helped you since

•

  avec don de parole
j'aurais pu te faire
    toi,   l'enfant de l'œ.
  roi faire de toi
      au lieu
— non, triste du fils
      en nous
  — te faire — de
      tâche
    non —
      or il
souviens-toi des prouve
      qui'il le
jours mauvais — fut —
      joua
bouche fermée, etc. ce rôle!
    parole
— etc. natale —
      oubliée
c'est moi qui
t'ai aidé depuis

(2

— have carried in
you the child —
   youth or curse
  of the story learned
    forgotten   from which
                       nothing

  I would not have
suffered — to be
in my turn
studying only that
— etc. (death

•

                  (2

— ai ramené en
toi l'enfant —
   jeunesse ou mal
  de l'histoire apprise
    oubliée   d'où
                    rien

  je n'aurais pas
souffert — en être
à mon tour
n'étudier que cela
— etc. (mort

24

(3
then — you would not then have been
    other than myself
    — since I am
here — alone, sad —
— no, I
    remember a
    childhood —
       — yours
         two voices)

---

but without you
I have not — known

•

(3
alors — tu ne fus
    donc que moi
    — puisque je suis
ici — seul, triste —
— non, je me
    souviens d'une
    enfance —
       — la tienne
         deux voix)

---

mais sans toi
je n'eusse — su

(4
before doing the
  +   )
⟨thus it is⟩
  thus it is me,
cursed hands —
who has bequeathed you!
    — silence
    (he forgives)

•

(4
avant de faire des
  +   )
⟨ainsi c'est⟩
  ainsi c'est moi,
mains maudites —
qui t'ai légué!
    — silence
    (il pardonne)

26

(5

Oh! leave... us
on this word
  — which mingles
the two of us
together
  — unites us
finally —
    for who said
it
        yours)

•

(5
Oh! laisse... nous
sur ce mot
  — qui nous
confond tous
deux
  — nous unit
enfin —
    car qui l'a
dit
        la tienne)

(1

cruel
etc.
   trappings
Oh! allow — no
you still want...

ancient egypt —
embalmings —
days, operations
crypts — all this
change

•

(1

manifestations
etc.
   cruelles
Oh! permets — non
tu veux encore...

egypte ancienne —
embaumements —
jours, opérations
cryptes — tout ce
changement

28

(2

once barbarous and
external
matter —
now
moral

and within us

•

(2

jadis barbare et
matériel
extérieur —
maintenant
moral

et en nous

                        want
            to thwart death
            ———

⟨Oh⟩ listen the woman
              her tears
Oh! I see
that you are strong, clever —
      etc.

•

                              veux
            déjouer mort
            ———

⟨Oh⟩ entends pleurs
              de femme
Oh! je le reconnais
tu es forte, habile —
      etc.

30

brother sister
not ever the absent one
———

will not be less than
the one present —

•

frère sœur
non jamais l'absent
———

ne sera moins que
le présent —

to feel it burst
⟨the vo⟩ in the night
the immense void
produced by what
would be his <u>life</u>
— because he <u>does</u> not
<u>know</u> it —
that he is dead
lightning?
attack
pain

31

•

sentir éclater
⟨le vi⟩ en nuit
le vide immense
produit par ce
qui serait sa <u>vie</u>
— parce qu'il <u>ne</u>
le <u>sait</u> pas —
qu'il est mort
éclair?
crise
douleur

32

(1

moment when we must
break with the
living memory,
to bury it
— put it in the coffin,
hide it — with
the brutalities of
putting it into the coffin
raw contact, etc.

•

(1

moment où il faut
rompre avec le
souvenir vivant,
pour l'ensevelir
— le mettre en bière,
le cacher — avec
les brutalités de
la mise en bière
contact rude, etc.

so as not to see it anymore
  except idealized —
afterwards, no longer him
alive there — but
seed of his being
taken back into itself —
seed allowing
to think for him
— to see him ⟨and to⟩

•

pour ne plus le voir
  qu'idéalisé —
après, non plus lui
vivant là — mais
germe de son être
repris en soi —
germe permettant
de penser pour lui
— de le voir ⟨et de⟩

34

vision (ideality
of the state) and to
speak for him
—

for in us, pure
him, purification
— become our
honor, the source
of our finest
feelings — etc

•

vision (idéalité
de l'état) et de
parler pour lui
—

car en nous, pur
lui, épuration
— devenu notre
honneur, la source
de nos meilleurs
sentiments — etc

(4

[+ true return
into the ideal]

_____

•

(4

[+ vraie rentrée
en l'idéal]

_____

treacherous blow
of death — of
<u>evil</u> without his
      <u>knowing</u> anything
— in my turn
to play with it, even
though the child knows
nothing

•

coup de traîtrise
de mort — du
<u>mal</u> sans qu'il en
      <u>sache</u> rien
— à mon tour
à la jouer, par
cela même qu'enfant
ignore

time of the
empty room
—
until we
open it
perhaps all
follows from this
(morally)

―――

•

temps de la
chambre vide
—
jusqu'à ce qu'on
l'ouvre
peut-être tout
suivre ainsi
(moralement)

―――

38

he knows nothing of it!
— and mother weeps —
idea there
yes, let us take everything
on ourselves, then his
life — etc. —
for sinister
not to know
and to be no more.

—

·

il n'en sait rien!
— et mère pleure —
idée là
oui, prenons tout
sur nous, alors sa
vie — etc. —
car sinistre
ne pas savoir
et n'être plus.

—

you can, with your little
hands, drag me
into your grave — you
have the right —
— I
who follow you, I
let myself go —
— but if you
wish, the two
  of us, let us make..

•

tu peux, avec tes
petites mains, m'entraîner
dans ta tombe — tu
en as le droit —
— moi-même
qui te suis moi, je
me laisse aller —
— mais si tu
veux, à nous
  deux, faisons..

40

an alliance
a hymen, superb
— and the life
remaining in me
I will use for – – – – –

and no mother
then?

•

(2
une alliance
un hymen, superbe
— et la vie
restant en moi
je m'en servirai
pour – – – – –

donc pas mère
alors?

(I

ceremony —
    casket —
    etc.
    we saw there (the father)
    the whole material side
— which allows us to
say is required —
    ah! yes! all
is there — ⟨and perhaps⟩
no fear for me
to think of something else
(the reformation

•

(I

cérémonie —
    cercueil —
    etc.
    on a vu là (le père)
    tout le côté matériel
— qui permet de se
dire au besoin —
    eh! bien oui! tout
est là — ⟨et peut-être⟩
pas de crainte pour moi
de penser à autre chose
(la reformation

42

of his spirit that is
eternal — can
wait

⌈ be but eternity
⌊ throughout my life

———

father —
to create his spirit
(he absent, alas!
as we would have
formed him present
——— better

but

•

de son esprit qui a
l'éternité — peut
attendre

⌈ soit mais éternité
⌊ à travers ma vie

———

père —
former son esprit
(lui absent, hélas!
comme on l'eût
formé lui présent
——— mieux

mais

sometimes when all
seems to go
too well — thus in
ideal —
  to cry out   —   ⟨it is not⟩
  in the mother's tone, who she
has become attentive —
It is not all that, no
I want him, him — and

      ———

not myself —

•

parfois quand tout
semble trop bien
aller — ainsi en
idéal —
  s'écrier   —   ⟨ce n'est⟩
  du ton de mère, qui elle
est devenue attentive —
Ce n'est pas tout cela
je le veux, lui — et

      ———

non moi —

44

(1

you look at me
I still cannot tell you
the truth
        I do not dare, too little one
What has happened to you
—

one day I will
tell you
        — for <u>man</u>
I do not want

•

(1

tu me regardes
Je ne peux pas te dire
encore la vérité
        je n'ose, trop petit
Ce qui t'est arrivé
—

un jour je te le
dirai
        — car <u>homme</u>
je ne veux pas

(2

you not to know
your fate
—

and man
dead child

•

(2

que tu ne saches
pas ton sort
—

et homme
enfant mort

46

no — nothing
to do with the great
deaths — etc.
— as long as we
go on living, he
lives — in us
—

it will only be after our
death that he will be dead
— and the bells
of the Dead will toll for
him

•

non — pas
mêlé aux grands
morts — etc.
— tant que nous
mêmes vivons, il
vit — en nous
—

ce n'est qu'après notre
mort qu'il en sera
— et que les cloches
des Morts sonneront pour
lui

      (1

little
   virgin
   betrothed life
   that would have been
   a woman
—

that I count for you
among all
you lack
  — but

           •

        (1

petite
   vierge
   fiancée vie
   qui eût été
   une femme
—

que je te conte
ce à quoi tu
manques
  — mais

48

Oh! leave
us   cemetery
father
— and let us speak
of what
the two of us
    know
        mystery

•

Oh! laissez
nous   cimetière
père
— et conversons
de ce qu'à
nous deux
    nous savons
        mystère

sail —
    navigates
    river,
your life that
goes by, that flows

—

49

•

voile —
    navigue
    fleuve,
ta vie qui
passe, coule

—

50

Oh! make us
                    suffer
    you who do not
    doubt it
much — all
that ⟨he⟩ equals
your life, painful in
            broken
us
—

    while
    you glide, free

•

Oh! fais-nous
                    souffrir
    toi qui ne t'en
    doutes pas
beaucoup — tout ce
qui ⟨il⟩ équivaut à
ta vie, douloureuse en
            brisée
nous
—

    tandis qu'alors
    tu planes, libre

What! this day of
the dead — for him —
him —

●

Quoi! ce jour des
morts — pour lui —
lui —

52

The sacrifice
    of the child

so that earth
   — mother — task
city men

•

Le sacrifice
    de l'enfant

pour que terre
   — mère — tâche
cité hommes

end of I
— o terror
he is dead!

he is... dead
(absolutely —
i.e. struck
the mother sees him in such

a way that,
sick, he seems
to come back — in the future —
or their race secured
in the present

•

fin de I
— o terreur
il est mort!

il est... mort
(absolument —
c. à. d. frappé
la mère le voit tel

de façon à ce que,
malade, il semble
revenir — en le futur —
ou leur race obtenu
au présent

54

mother I
one cannot
die with such
eyes, etc.

———

father lets escape
in his horror,
sobs
      "he is dead"
— and it is in the wake
of this cry, that
II the child

•

mère I
on ne peut pas
mourir avec de pareils
yeux, etc.

———

père laisse entendre
en son effroi,
sanglots
      «il est mort»
— et c'est en vague
de ce cri, que
II l'enfant se

stands up on his bed
he looks, etc.
—

  in III perhaps
nothing — ⟨positive⟩
            on death
and
  simply
stated — in
  the space of "he is
    dead of I II
    ——

•

lève sur son lit
il cherche, etc.
—

  en III peut-être
rien — ⟨d'affirmé⟩
           sur mort
et
  donné à entendre
simplement — en
  l'espace de «il est
    mort de I II
    ——

56

The father looks —
and stops —
the child being
there, still, as if
to take hold of life again
— now interruption
in the father — and the
mother appearing hopes
cares —   the double side
              man woman
              — soon in
profound union
              the one, in the other, from which

•

Le père cherche —
et s'arrête —
l'enfant étant
là, encore, comme
pour ressaisir la vie
— or interruption
chez le père — et la
mère apparue espoirs
soins —   le double côté
              homme femme
              — tantôt chez
union profonde
              l'un, chez l'autre, d'où

(1

and you his sister,
you who one day
— (this gulf open
since his death and
that will follow us
until our own —
when we will
have descended there
your mother and I)
must one day

•

(1

et toi sa sœur,
toi qui un jour
— (ce gouffre ouvert
depuis sa mort et
qui nous suivra
jusqu'à la nôtre —
quand nous y
serons descendus
ta mère et moi)
dois un jour

58

unite all three
of us in your thought,
you memory — — —
   —   just as in
      a single tomb
  you who, following
the order, will come
upon this tomb, not
made for you —

●

nous réunir tous
trois en ta pensée,
ta mémoire — — —
   —   de même qu'en
      une seule tombe
  toi qui, selon
l'ordre, viendras
sur cette tombe, non
faite pour toi —

Setting sun
and wind
  now vanished, and
wind of <u>nothing</u>
<u>that breathes</u>
(here, the modern
? nothingness)

•

Soleil couché
et vent
  or parti, et
vent de <u>rien</u>
<u>qui souffle</u>
(là, le néant
? moderne)

60

tears, influx
                    the
of lucidity, dead one
is seen again
sheer through

———

•

larmes, afflux
                    le
de lucidité, mort
se revoit à
travers

———

(1

death — whispers softly
— I am no one—
I do not even know who I am
(for the dead do not
know they are
dead —, nor even that they
die
— for children
at least
— or

•

(1

la mort — chuchotte bas
— je ne suis personne —
je m'ignore même
(car morts ne savent
pas qu'ils sont
morts —, ni même qu'ils
meurent
— pour enfants
du moins
— ou

62

heroes — sudden
deaths

for otherwise
my beauty is
made of last
moments —
lucidity, beauty
face — of
what would be

•

héros — morts
soudaines

car autrement
ma beauté est
faite des derniers
instants —
lucidité, beauté
visage — de
ce qui serait

(3
me, without myself
—

for as soon as
            (as one is
I am — ⟨I⟩
dead) I cease
to be —

—

thus made of
forebodings, of in-
tuitions, supreme

•

(3
moi, sans moi
—

car aussitôt que
                (qu'on est
je suis — ⟨je⟩
mort) je cesse
d'être —

—

ainsi faite de
presciences, d'in-
tuitions, frissons

64

(4
shudders — I
am not —
        but at the ideal
    state
———

and for the
others, tears
mourning, etc —

and it is my

•

                    (4
suprêmes — je
ne suis pas —
            qu'à l'état
        idéal
    ———

et pour les
autres, larmes
deuil, etc —

et c'est mon

⟨5

shadow not knowing
of myself, who
dresses in mourning

——————

the others —

——————

⟨tears, no more⟩
—————— ⟨nor⟩
⟨others⟩ — — —
⟨from which came⟩

•

⟨5

ombre ignorance
de moi, qui
revêt de deuil

——————

les autres —

——————

⟨larmes, plus de⟩
—————— ⟨ni de⟩
⟨autres⟩ — — —
⟨d'où venue⟩

66

Notes
———

whatever poem
based on facts
always — should
take only
general facts —
it happens here
that taken to-
gether harmonize

•

Notes
———

quoique poëme
basé sur faits
toujours — doive
ne prendre que
faits généraux —
il se trouve ici
que donnée d'en-
semble s'accorde

often with the
last ⟨destiny⟩ moments of the
delightful child —

thus father —
    seeing that he
    must be dead

—

      mother, supreme
      illusion, etc.

•

souvent avec les
moments ⟨destin⟩ derniers du
délicieux enfant —

ainsi père —
    voyant qu'il
    doit être mort

—

      mère, illusion
      suprême, etc.

68

death — purification
image in ourselves
purified by   ⎡and before
                   ⎢image
tears   ——   ⎣also —
simply remains
not to touch —
but to speak —

•

mort — épuration
image en nous
épurés par   ⎡et avant
                ⎢image
larmes   ——   ⎣aussi —
reste simplement
ne pas toucher —
mais se parler —

(I

II general effect
⟨he must⟩
is he dead? (i.
e. struck to death
⟨no⟩
     and is he coming back already
(in the space of the
must die)
          from the terrible future
that awaits him?

•

(I

II effet général
⟨il doit⟩
est-il mort? (c. à
d. frappé à mort)
⟨non⟩
     et revient-il déjà
(dans l'espace du
doit mourir?
          du futur terrible
qui l'attend?

⟨II⟩   (2

70

or is he
still sick?

—

sickness one
clings
to, want-
ing it
to last, to have him
longer

—

now <u>death</u>

•

⟨II⟩   (2
ou bien est-il
encore malade?

—

maladie à la-
quelle on se
rattache, dési-
rant qu'elle
dure, pour l'avoir,
lui plus longtemps

—

or la <u>mort</u>

(3

"why stop me
from making you
worried — sad —
distorted — while
I mold it
for the beautiful and sacred
day when he will not
suffer anymore —   [on the

•

(3
«pourquoi m'attarder
à vous le rendre
inquiet — triste —
déformé — tandis
que je le pétris
pour le jour
beau et sacré
où il ne souffrira
plus —   [sur le

72

death bed —
⟨he who⟩ but
mute, etc. — instead
of formerly I —
perhaps what
will go in I —
  "Oh! if he would never
die — — — — —
        mother

•

lit de mort —
⟨ce qui se⟩ mais
muet, etc. — au lieu
d'autrefois I —
ce qui donnerait
peut-être pour I —
  "Oh! s'il mourait
jamais — — — — —
        mère

(5
does not end —
— the father and mother
are needed?
　　who both find
themselves before
sepulchre — without him
ah! well —?

•

(5
n'achève pas —
— il faut le père
et mère?
　　qui se retrouvent
tous deux devant
sépulcre — sans lui
eh! bien —?

                              (I
                  seated, dreamer
74   ⟨not to⟩   talking
                              with him
        not to feel you on
        my knees, that
        means they slip away
        and that I am
        kneeling
              — no longer before
        the familiar child
        etc. — then, with
                  ⟨but the⟩

                                    •

                                    (I
                        assis, rêveur
        ⟨ne pas⟩   causant
                              avec lui
            ne pas te sentir sur
        mes genoux, cela
        fait qu'ils se dérobent
        et que je me suis
        agenouillé
              — non plus devant
        l'enfant familier
        etc. — alors, avec
                  ⟨mais le⟩

(2
his jacket — (sailor?)
but before
the young god,
hero, made holy through
death —

•

(2
sa veste — (marin?)
mais devant
le jeune dieu,
héros, sacré par
mort —

family perfect
balance
    father son
    mother daughter

broken —
three, a void
among us,
      searching…

•

famille parfaite
équilibre
    père fils
    mère fille

rompu —
trois, un vide
entre nous,
      cherchant…

much better
that he not know it
    —
    we take on all
    tears
        — weep, mother
    etc.
— transition from one
    state to the other
        thus not dead
death — ridiculous enemy
    —who cannot inflict on the child
        the notion that you exist!

•

    tant mieux
qu'il ne le sache pas
    —
    nous prenons toutes
    larmes
        — pleure, mère
    etc.
— transition d'un
    état à l'autre
        ainsi pas mort
mort — ridicule ennemie
    — qui ne peux à l'enfant
        infliger la notion que tu es!

death is not   prayer
                of mother
nothing   — playing
                death
    〈remedies〉   she
    "so that the child
    does not
        know

—

and father benefits.

•

mort n'est   prière
                de mère
rien   — jouant
                    mort
    〈remèdes〉   elle
    «que l'enfant
    ne sache
        pas

—

et père en profite.

no more life for

—

me
    and I feel
I am lying in the grave
beside you.

•

plus de vie pour

—

moi
    et je me sens
couché en la tombe
à côté de toi.

or: ordinary
Poem

It is true
you have struck me
and you have carefully chosen
your wound —
— etc.
— but
_____

and vengeance
struggle between spirit and
death

•

.

ou: Poème
ordinaire

C'est vrai
tu m'as frappé
et tu as bien choisi
ta blessure —
— etc.
— mais
_____

et vengeance
lutte d'un génie et de
la mort

death
there are only conso-
lations, thoughts — balm

but what is done
is done — we cannot
hark back to the absolute
stuff of death —

— and nevertheless
to show that if,
once life has been

•

mort
il n'est que des conso-
lations, pensées — baume

mais ce qui est fait
est fait — on ne peut
revenir sur l'absolu
contenu en mort —

— et cependant
montrer que si,
abstraction faite

•

82

abstracted, the happiness of being
together, etc — this
consolation in its turn,
has its foundation — its base —
absolute — in what
(if we ⟨ma⟩ want
for example that a
dead being lives in
us, thought —
it is his being, his

•

de vie, de bonheur d'être
ensemble, etc — cette
consolation a son tour,
a son fonds — sa base —
absolus — en ce que
(si nous ⟨fai⟩ voulons
par exemple qu'un
être mort vive en
nous, pensée —
c'est son être, sa

(3

thought in fact —
what is best in him
that happens, through our
love and the care
we take
of his being —
    [being, not being
        more than moral and
            as for thought]

in this there is
a magnificent beyond

•

(3

pensée en effet —
ce qu'il a de meilleur
qui arrive, par notre
amour et le soin
que nous prenons
à l'être —
    [être, n'étant
        que moral et
            quant à pensée]

il y a là un au
delà magnifique

84

(4

that rediscovers its
truth — so much more
pure and beautiful than
the absolute break
of death — little by little
become as illusory
as absolute (from which one is
allowed to seem
to <u>forget</u> the pains
etc —)

•

(4

qui retrouve sa
vérité — d'autant plus
pure et belle que
la rupture absolue de
la mort — devenue
peu à peu aussi illusoire
qu'absolue (d'où il est
permis de paraître
<u>oublier</u> les douleurs
etc —)

⟨5

— just as this illu-
sion of survival in
us, becomes the absolute
illusion — (there is ⟨being⟩
unreality in the two
cases) was terrible
    and true,

———

85

•

⟨5

— comme cet illu-
soire de survie en
nous, devient d'illusoire
absolu — (il y a ⟨être⟩
irréalité dans les deux
cas) a été terrible
    et vraie,

———

86 —

the father alone
    the mother alone

    each hiding from
    the other
    and found again

    —

———

together

•

le père seul
    la mère seule
—

    se cachant l'un
    de l'autre
    et cela se retrouve

    —

———

ensemble

o earth — you do not
   grow anything
— pointless
— I who
   honor you —

bouquets
   vain beauty

•

ô terre — tu n'as
   pas une plante
— à quoi bon —
— moi qui
   t'honore —

bouquets
   vaine beauté

friends
    mysterious finger
shown

    appeared
— chasing away
    the false

———

88

•

les amis
    doigt mystérieux
montré

    apparus
— chassant
    les faux

———

⟨little⟩

of vain

source

stays there —   dead?

be!

and that life will pass

———— river

beside him

protected by harsh nature

_____

the little one fallen

into the valley

•

⟨petit⟩

de source

vaine

reste là —   mort?

soit!

et que la vie passe

———— fleuve

à côté de lui

gardé par nature sévère

_____

le petit tombé dans

la vallée

90

purity
double
— identity
—

the eyes
the two points of
equal sight

•

pureté
double
— identité
—

les yeux
les deux points de
vue égaux

his eyes look
at me, double
  and sufficient
  — already claimed by
absence and the
    gulf

—

everything comes together there?

•

ses yeux me
regardent, doubles
  et suffisent
  — pris déjà par
l'absence et le
    gouffre

—

tout y raccorder?

92

(1

man and
absence —
   the twin
spirit he unites
with when he
dreams, longs

— absence, alone
after death, once

•

(1

l'homme et
l'absence —
   l'esprit
jumeau avec lequel
il s'unit quand il
rêve, songe

— absence, seule
après mort, une

(2

the pious
burial of the
body, makes myste-
riously — this
admitted fiction —

•

(2

fois le pieux
enfouissement du
corps, fait mysté-
rieusement — cette
fiction accordée —

The sacrifice —
        on the tomb
why + , love
        mother
    it is necessary
        — so that he might be
again! (transfusion)
        mother alone wants
            to have him, she is earth
                —

•

Le sacrifice —
        sur le tombeau
pourquoi + , amour
        mère
    il le faut
        — pour qu'il soit
encore! (transfusion)
        mère veut seule
            l'avoir, elle est terre
                —

Since it is necessary
What are you saying there —
do not interrupt me —

•

Puisqu'il faut
Que dis-tu là —
ne m'interromps point —

96

I

mother's fears
— he stopped
playing
today

father listens — sees
the mother's eyes
— allows to be cared for II
and dreams
—

•

I

craintes de mère
— il a cessé
de jouer
aujourd'hui

père écoute — voit
yeux de mère
— laisse soigner II
et songe lui
—

II

mother's tears
   room
little by little calming down
  in the double
  point of view
    child, destiny
  —

  tomb, memory
old man —
    — (who speaks)

•

II

larmes de mère
   pièce
se calmant peu à peu
  dans le double
  point de vue
    enfant, destinée
  —

  tombeau, souvenir
vieillard —
    — (qui parle)

98

I   mother's cry
flowers
   gathered for
      tomb, left there

III
tomb
   father —

•

I   cri de mère
fleurs
   cueillies pour
      tombe, laissées là

III
tombeau
   père —

slow to sacrifice
earth alters him
during this time

other mother
(mother says nothing?)

mute and eternal
pain.

•

lent à sacrifice
terre le change
pendant ce temps

autre mère
(mère se tait?)

douleur éternelle
et muette.

(I

if he had heard us
whether he would have been made worse

—

to suppress it
thus
sacrilege without
                              tomb
that he know it!   shadow

—

no, divinely
          for not dead
and in us
                    — the

●

                              (I
s'il nous entendait
qu'il serait irrité

—

le supprimer
ainsi
sacrilège sans
                              tombeau
qu'il le sache!   ombre

—

non, divinement
          car pas mort
et en nous
                    — la

transfusion —
   change in the manner
   of being, that's all

•

transfusion —
   changement de mode
   d'être, voilà tout

102

what!
to rejoice in
presence
and to forget him
when absent
— simply! ingratitude!
no — "hold" on
the life" of the being
who was — absolute
—

•

quoi!
jouir de la
présence
et l'oublier
absent
— simplement! ingratitude!
non — «prise» sur
l'être» de qui a
été — absolu
—

Bitterness and
need for revenge
when he
seems to protest
———
desire to do
nothing anymore — ⟨nothing⟩
to miss the sublime
goal, etc. —

•

Amertume et
besoin de vengeance
quand il
semble réclamer
———
désir de ne plus
rien faire — ⟨rien⟩
manquer le but
sublime, etc. —

what! enormous
   death — terrible
   death
   —

   to strike down
      so small a creature
   —
I say to death   coward

   alas! it is within us
   not without

·

quoi! la mort
   énorme — la
      terrible mort
   —
   frapper un si
      petit être
   —
je dis à la mort   lâche

   hélas! elle est en nous
   non le dehors

he has dug our
grave
in dying

has granted it

`

•

il a creusé notre
tombe
en mourant

concession

III

Friend
—
     the friend — — — —
burial   to the vision of
                the child
   you alone do not know it —
—   you look at me
   how are   still
              stunned
   you — close these sweet eyes
   — not know — I
   take care of it —   continue
    and you will live —

•

III

Ami
—
     l'ami — — — —
ensevelissement à la vision de
              l'enfant
   toi seul ne le sais pas —
—   tu me regardes
   comment te   toujours
             étonné
   va — ferme ces doux yeux
   — ne sache pas — je me
   charge —   continue
   et tu vivras —

    to see him <u>dead</u>
— the mother's fears
        on the funeral bed
  from the moment the playing
    stopped in I
    — end of I
      break
 voice that cries until
that — for the mute child

·

    le voir <u>mort</u>
— craintes de la mère
       sur lit funéraire
  dès la cessation de
    jeux en I
    — fin de I
      rupture
 voix qui crie jusque
là — pour l'enfant muet

108

(2

and to join — eyes
closed — father —
(mother closed them —
"not to know where he
is", to bury him in
the shadow
— struggle, stuggle
—

•

(2

et relier — yeux fer-
més — père —
(mère les a fermés —
«ne pas savoir où il
est», l'enterrer dans
l'ombre
— lutte, lutte
—

Oh! that the eyes of the dead
etc.
    have more strength
than those, the most beautiful eyes
of the living
    —

        that they would lure you in

        — —

•

        Oh! que les yeux des morts
etc.
        ont plus de force
que ceux, les plus beaux
des vivants
    —

        qu'ils vous attireraient

        — —

110

Breaking off from I
to III
child dies then

III   (to speak
often to him
I take you my child,
—

room ardent thought
—burial
in — — —

II tears of the two
hidden
I and   one from the other

•

Scission de I
à III
enfant mort là

III   (s'adresser
souvent à lui
je te prends mon enfant,
—

chambre ardente pensée
—ensevelissement
en — — —

II larmes des deux
cachées
I et   l'un à l'autre

III
tomb — ⟨goes⟩ fatality
— father — "he had
    to die — "
    mother does not want
    anyone to talk like this
    about her flower —
— and father returns
to fulfilled des-
tiny in the form
            of the child

•

III
tombeau — ⟨va⟩ fatalité
— père — «il devait
    mourir — »
    mère ne veut pas
    qu'on parle ainsi
    de son fruit —
— et père revient
à destinée accom-
plie en tant
            qu'enfant

III

112   earth speaks —
            mother confused with
         earth
         through ditch dug
               by child — where
            she will be — — —
               later —

·

III

terre parle —
      mère confondue à
terre
par fosse creusée
      par enfant — où
   elle sera — — —
      plus tard —

child
sister remains, who
will lead to a future
brother
    — she exempt from
this grave for
father mother and son
— by her marriage.

•

    enfant
sœur reste, qui
amènera un frère
futur
    — elle exempte de
cette tombe pour
père mère et fils
— par son mariage.

114

suffering — not vain
tears — falling
in ignorance — but
emotion, ⟨you n⟩ nourish-
ing your shadow
that comes to life in us

———

setting it up

———

life-giving tribute
  for him —

•

douleur — non larmes
vaines — tombant
en ignorance — mais
émotion, ⟨te n⟩ nourris-
sant ton ombre
qui se vivifie en nous

———

l'installant

———

tribut vivifiant
  pour lui —

don't cry so loudly
   he will hear —

———

daughter struck dumb

•

ne pleure pas si haut
   il entendrait —

———

fille frappée de stupeur

116

What! was he born then for
                    mother
    not being   too beautiful
                            too
    and the father's terror
    cursing his blood

    — the mother — yes, made
    for being, his eyes — to what
    good such worry —
        he will live! (last cry)
                    treatments, etc.

        at least death
    takes the meaning that he

                    •

        Quoi! était-il donc né pour
                        mère
        ne pas être   trop beau
                                trop
            et effroi chez le père
            maudissant son sang

            — la mère — si, fait
            pour être, ses yeux — à quoi
            bon tant d'inquiétude —
                il vivra! (cri dernier)
                            soins, etc.

                au moins mort
            prends le sens qu'il

(2
        or mother
knows it
        (sometimes, he turns away
        from me,

        and such terrible sacrifice

— father will unite
everything later in
        prolonging
            his being,
                reabsorbing
                    etc.

                    •

                                    (2
                        ou mère
    le sache
        (parfois, il se détourne
        de moi,

            et si terrible sacrifice

— père raccordera
tout plus tard en
        prolongeant
            son être,
                résorbant
                    etc.

118

Silent father
     opening of thought
—

oh! the horrible secret
I carry inside me
     (what to do about it

—

will become
     the shadow of his
          tomb
not known —

—

     that he must
          die

•

Père silencieux
     début de pensée
—

oh! l'horrible secret
dont je suis possesseur
     (qu'en faire

—

deviendrai
     l'ombre de son
          tombeau
non su —

—

     qu'il doit
          mourir

after-effect
  ⟨immortality⟩
    eternity
  ⟨pre⟩ thanks to
  our love
— he prolongs us
  beyond

      —

      (in exchange
      we give him back
        life

  in filling ourselves
    with thought

•

contrecoup
  ⟨immortalité⟩
    éternité
  ⟨pre⟩grâce à
  notre amour
— il nous prolonge
  au delà

      —

      (en échange
      nous lui
        rendons vie

  en nous faisant
    penseur

tenderly: we must not
cry anymore
120 let us cry no more
look at you
man
— I can tell you
what you do not know
that you were betrayed —
falsehood, etc —

---

old +
god of his race
— as poet
— the one who not
— as man
stirs
each of our gestures
etc.
— gold!

•

tendrement: il ne faut
plus pleurer
ne pleurons plus
te voici
homme
— je puis te dire
ce que tu ne sais pas
que tu fus trahi —
mensonge, etc —

---

vieux +
dieu de sa race
— comme poète
— celui qui pas
— comme homme
remue
chacun de nos gestes
etc.
— l'or!

                    after, no you will not
                              take him
Yes—   (1

                    121
            I recognize
         your power o death

         stealthily
              — you took him —
         he is now only spirit
         in us — etc.
powerless against human kind
         but   human death
         as long as humanity
         century stone tomb

                    •

                              après, non tu ne le
                                        prendras pas
                    Oui —   (1
                         je reconnais
                    ta puissance ô mort

                    en les dessous
                         — tu l'as pris —
                    il n'est plus qu'esprit
                    en nous — etc.
         impuissante contre le génie humain
                    mais   mort humain
                    tant qu'humanité
                    siècle pierre tombeau

(stop
earth — open ditch
never to be filled
   — except by sky
   — indifferent earth
  grave
    not flowers
bouquets, our
festivals and our life

•

(cesse
terre — trou ouvert et
jamais comblé
   — que par ciel
   — terre indifférente
  tombe
    non fleurs
bouquets, nos
fêtes et notre vie

little child
that death can take
the ignorant
— but young
afflicted man — already
in him — I do not dare
endure this look
filled with the future
— oh! good, <u>evil</u>

•

petit enfant
que mort peut prendre
l'ignorant
— mais jeune
homme irrité — déjà
en lui — je n'ose
soutenir ce regard
plein de futur
— eh! bien, <u>mal</u>

124

race in
     me —
   that this look
follows beyond into
(absolute) future
our reunion

―――

must it —
     by what ritual?
   to inhume in the name
of race, ancestors, with

•

de race dans
     moi —
   que ce regard
suit au delà en
futur (absolu)
notre réunion

―――

faut-il —
     selon quel rite?
   l'inhumer en nom
de race, ancêtres, avec

immortality ⁽3
— or mine
new —

•

immortalité ⁽3
— ou le mien
nouveau —

126

cemetery
the need to go there
to renew
    laceration
pain — through
     the dear being
idea of ⟨death⟩ there

———

  when the too powerful
illusion of having him
always with us

no, you are not one of the dead
  — you will not be among
the dead, always in us

•

cimetière
nécessaire d'y aller
pour renouveler
    déchirure
douleur — par
     l'être cher
idée de ⟨mort⟩ là

———

  quand l'illusion
trop forte de l'avoir
toujours avec soi

non, tu n'es pas un mort
  — tu ne seras pas parmi
les morts, toujours en nous

(2

becomes a
delight (bitter enough
point) for us —
and unjust for the one
who remains below, and is
in reality deprived
of all that
we connect him with.

———

•

(2

devient une
jouissance (point assez
amère) pour nous —
et injuste pour celui
qui reste là bas, et est
en réalité privé
de tout ce à quoi
nous l'associons.

———

128

mother identity
        of dead life
                father picks up
rhythm started here
of mother's
 rocking
    suspense — life
     death —
poetry — thought

·

mère identité
        de vie mort
                père reprend
rythme pris ici
du bercement de
mère
    suspens — vie
      mort —
poésie — pensée

no death — you will not
deceive him —
— I take advantage of the fact
that you deceive him
— for his happy
　　ignorance
　　— but on the other hand
I take it back from you
　　for the ideal tomb

•

non mort — tu ne le
tromperas pas —
— je profite de
ce que tu le trompes
— pour son heureuse
　　ignorance à lui
　　— mais d'autre part
je te le reprends
　　pour le tombeau idéal

130

(2

I want to suffer everything
⟨— ain⟩ for you
   who do not know —
   nothing will be
taken away (but
you) from the hideous mourning

— — —

and it's me, the man
you would have been

——

— for I will, from

•

(2

je veux tout souffrir
⟨— ain⟩ pour toi
   qui ignores —
   rien ne sera
soustrait (qu'à
toi) du deuil inoui

— — —

et c'est moi, l'homme
que tu eusses été

——

— car je vais, à

(3

this mo-
ment on ⟨the⟩ <u>be you</u>
— —

father and mother
  together
    their love

    idea of the child

to mother
  yes, weep
    — I however think

•

(3

dater de main-
tenant ⟨l'⟩ <u>t'être</u>
— —

père et mère à
  deux
    leur amour

    idée de l'enfant

à mère
  pleure toi
    — moi, je pense

132

Tomb
—

I. what!... here the sob
  the indignant protest
        hurled out to infinity
II. to take on oneself
  all his suffering
        middle —
and III. then, one can, eyes
  lifted to the sky —

————————————

draw the final line, the calm
of the heavy tomb —

•

Tombeau
—

I. quoi!... ici le sanglot
  la protestation indignée
        projetée à l'infini
II. prendre sur soi
  toutes ses souffrances
        moyen —
et III. alors, on peut, yeux
  levés au ciel —

————————————

tirer la ligne finale, et calme
du lourd tombeau —

—
gravely —
such a painful thing
before ————
but not without
(sacrifice of
delights?) again
throwing on this
⟨rigid⟩ sinister line
of erasure
the last lamented flowers
once meant for him

•

—
gravement —
chose si pénible
avant ————
mais non sans
(sacrifice de
jouissances?) jeter
encore sur cette
ligne ⟨rigid⟩ sinistre
et d'effacement
les dernières fleurs
jadis pour lui regrettées

134

(1

Indeed Sir
    indeed you are
        death
At least that
is what your announcement
letter

———

  and laughter from within
  myself — hideous!
in writing this as
your faithful servant —
    you who will see
clearly, o my — dearly

•

(1

Oui Monsieur
  oui vous êtes
    mort
C'est ainsi du moins
que votre lettre de
faire-part

———

  et rire au dedans
  de moi — affreux!
en écrivant ceci comme
le vôtre —
    vous qui verrez
bien, ô mon — bien

beloved — that
if I could not
embrace you
squeeze you in
my arms
— it is because you were
inside me

Dear companion of the
hours I used to call
bad, and no
less later of those
I later call

•

aimé — que
si je ne pouvais
vous étreindre
vous presser en
mes bras
— c'est que vous étiez
en moi

Cher compagnon des
heures que je disais
mauvaises, et non
moins plus tard de celles
que plus tard je dis

136

(ı

myself —
   perhaps —
the ambiguity
   this can produce!

•

(ı

moi —
   peut-être —
l'ambiguité
   que cela se puisse!

(2

pain ⟨and⟩ and sweet
delights
of the suffering
ghost

·

(2
peine ⟨et⟩ et jouissances
douces
du revenant
malade

138

mother
  he will not live!
———

two
—

father, in front of
    tomb
 (mother to side?
   then come back?
———————

•

mère
  il ne vivra pas!
———

deux
—

père, devant
    tombeau
 (écarte mère?
   puis revient?
———————

3rd part

  — the sacrificing father
    prepares himself —
  but idea remains and
    of him
  to construct everything on it —

     an offering to the absolute

●

3e partie

  — père sacrificateur
    se dispose —
  mais idée reste et
    de lui
  tout édifier là dessus —

      et offre à absolu

2nd part

140

bitter
　—ah! so much the better that
not man
　　　but his eyes...
　　　but his mouth
— who says this? perhaps
his lover.
—

o lover, daughter I would have
loved
—

to return to mother?

●

2ᵉ partie

amer
　— ah! tant mieux que
pas homme
　　　mais ses yeux...
　　　mais sa bouche
— que parle ainsi? peut-être
son amante.
—

ô amante, fille que j'eusse
aimée
—

revenir à mère?

2nd part

seen, come back dead, through
illness — eyes, want
to pour out light.
    — to pretend to agree
to play, with indifference

——

    he knows without knowing
    and we weep for him without
letting him know

    enough tears — it is
to introduce death —

•

2ᵉ partie

vu, revenu mort, à travers
maladie — yeux, veulent
bien verser le jour.
    — faire semblant consentir
à jouer, avec indifférence

——

    il sait sans savoir
    et nous le pleurons sans
le lui montrer

    assez de larmes — c'est
introduire la mort —

1st part

142 —

one feels — fatal blow
illuminating the soul —
that dead —
    and (thunder) everything that
tumbles down
    —

    dream of leaving him a name, etc.

•

1re partie

    —

on sent — coup fatal
illuminant l'âme —
que mort —
    et (tonnerre) tout ce
qui s'écroule
    —

    rêve de lui laisser un nom, etc.

    already so changed that
it is no longer him —
    and the <u>idea</u> (of him) <u>yes</u>!
in this way li<u>ttle</u> by little
comes through.

——————

later, from the moment
that death hovers ———

•

    déjà si changé que
ce n'est plus lui —
    et l'<u>idée</u> (de lui) <u>si</u>!
ainsi se dé<u>gage</u> peu
à peu.

——————

plus tard, du moment
que mort plane ———

144

sick
　　considered
　　　as dead
one already loves such an object
"who recalls it!"
　　　to set things in order

　　　————————

and sometimes hope
　　　blasts this fiction
　　　　　　of death
"no — he will live! —

·

　　　malade
　　　　considéré
　　　　　comme mort
on aime déjà tel objet
«qui le rappelle!»
　　　　ranger

　　　————————

et parfois espoir
　　　crève cette fiction
　　　　　　de mort
«non — il vivra! —

life sheltered in us
where our dread —
   horror of hole
      clings
   ———
to make this the sacrifice —
   —
or poems, for
later, after
us, death —
      being

•

vie réfugiée en nous
où la nôtre effroi —
   horreur de trou
      s'attache
   ———
en faire le sacrifice —
   —
ou poèmes, pour
plus tard, après
nous, mort —
      être

that future eyes
filled with earth
never
cloud over
with time

————

•

que jamais
yeux futurs,
pleins de terre
ne se
voilent de temps

————

I cannot believe
all this has
happened —
———— To
   begin again
in spirit beyond —
      the burial

                  etc —

•

Je ne peux pas croire
à tout ce qui s'est
passé —
———— Le
   recommencer en
esprit au delà —
      l'ensevelissement

                  etc —

death!
Oh! you believe that
you will take me
thus — to this
mother
 — to me
  father

———

I admit that you can
  do much

•

   mort!
Oh! tu crois que
tu me le prendras
ainsi — à cette
mère
 — à moi
  père

———

j'avoue que tu peux
  beaucoup

(1

what do you want, sweet
adored vision —
who often come
towards me and lean
over — as if
to listen to secret [of
my tears] —
to know that you are
dead
— what you do not know?
— no I will not

•

(1

que veux-tu, douce
vision adorée —
qui viens souvent
vers moi, te
pencher — comme
écouter secret [de
mes larmes] —
savoir que tu es
mort
— ce que tu ignores?
— non je ne

(2

150

tell it
to you — for then you
would disappear —
and I would be alone
weeping, for you, me,
mingled, you weeping for
                    child
in me
        the future
man you will not
be, and who remain
without life or joy.

•

                    (2
te le dirai
pas — car alors tu
disparaîtrais —
et je resterais seul
pleurant, toi, moi,
mêlé, toi te pleurant
                    enfant
en moi
        l'homme
futur que tu ne seras
pas, et qui reste
sans vie ni joie.

—
vision
endlessly purified
by my tears

———

•

—
vision
sans cesse épurée
par mes larmes

———

152

pro-
cess ⌈He, dead —
          ⟨seen⟩ so beautiful
⌊child
— and that the savage
              dread
of death fall on
him [disturbed by
mother's cry] with
the man he should have
become [seen in this
          supreme instant]

to render death bed

•

pro-
cédé ⌈Lui, mort —
          ⟨vu⟩ si beau,
⌊enfant
— et que l'effroi
              farouche
de mort tombe sur
lui [dérangé par
cri de mère] avec
l'homme qu'il eût
du être [vu en cet
          instant suprême]

pour rendre lit de mort

oh — provided
that he knows nothing
of it — does
not doubt

—

  [during sickness
— but from which treason
  unknown
    death —

•

oh — pourvu
qu'il n'en sache
rien — ne
se doute pas

—

  [pendant maladie
— mais d'où trahison
  la mort
    ignorée —

154

no, I can
not throw earth
of oblivion
— — —

[earth mother
     take him back
in your shadow
—

and his spirit
     in me as well]

mother has bled and wept
father sacrifices — and deifies

•

non, je ne
puis jeter terre
de l'oubli
— — —

[terre mère
     reprends le
en ton ombre
—

et de même son
     esprit en moi]

mère a saigné et pleuré
père sacrifie — et divinise

II

not me —
    in myself —
    ———

and absence —
———

oppos. IV or +
the always
    self, nothing
               that we
but self!   love —
torturing the delicate
    soul

155

•

II

pas moi —
    en moi —
    ———

et absence —
———

oppos. IV ou +
le toujours
    soi, rien
               qu'on
que soi!   aime —
torturant l'âme
    délicate

156

(1

imply
perhaps the
ceremony
— funeral
etc — in brief what
people saw —
(burial
   mass?

  to carry this

•

             (1

sous entendre
peut-être la
cérémonie
— pompes funèbres
etc — bref ce qu'a
vu le monde —
(enterrement
   messe?

  pour ramener

(2
to intimacy
— the room —
empty — absence —
open — the
moment when his
absence ends,
so that he may be
in us —
—

that will be this
3rd part —

•

(2
cela à l'intimité
— la chambre —
vide — absence —
ouverte — le
moment où son
absence finit,
pour qu'il soit
en nous —
—

ce serait cette
3ᵉ partie —

158

(3

after he has been
carried away, ⟨end of I⟩
out of the room —

— to see then
how II — "the
⟨which will be the⟩
⟨of⟩ sickness and
the little phantom" —
would be framed —
— III ghost

•

(3

après qu'il a été
enlevé, ⟨fin de I⟩
parti de la chambre —

— voir alors
comment II — «la
⟨quelle serait la⟩
⟨de⟩ maladie et
le petit fantôme» —
s'encadreraient —
— III revenant

(4
above, towards
the end of II —
dead —

in this way furniture
immortality
—

and heart of nature
I — he will not play
anymore — merging
with countryside
    where he rests?
—

•

(4
par dessus, vers
la fin de II —
mort —

ainsi meubles
immortalité
—

et fond de nature
I — il ne jouera
plus — se mêlant
à campagne
    où il repose?
—

to specify?

160

Ah! adorable heart
o my image
placed among the too vast
destinies —
    only a child
  like you —
       I dream
          still
   all alone — —
  in the future —

•

particulariser?

Ah! cœur adorable
ô mon image
là bas des trop grands
destins —
    qu'enfant
  comme toi —
       je rêve
          encore
   tout seul — —
  en l'avenir —

⟨1

Oh! you understand
that if I consent
to live — to seem
to forget you —
it is to ⟨so that⟩
feed my pain
— and so that this apparent
forgetfulness
    can spring forth more
horribly in tears, at

·

⟨1

Oh! tu sais bien
que si je consens
à vivre — à paraître
t'oublier —
c'est pour ⟨que⟩
nourrir ma douleur
— et que cet oubli
apparent
    jaillisse plus
vif en larmes, à

162

(2

some random
moment, in
the middle of this
life, when you
appear to me.

•

(2

un moment
quelconque, au
milieu de cette
vie, quand tu
m'y apparais

(I

time — that body
takes to decompose
in earth — (min-
gling little by little
with neutral earth
at the vast horizons)

it is then that he
lets go of the pure
spirit that we

163

•

(I

temps — que corps
met à s'oblitérer
en terre — (se con-
fondre peu à peu
avec terre neutre
aux vastes horizons)

c'est alors qu'il
lâche l'esprit
pur que l'on

164

were — and which was
tied to him, orga-
nized — which
can, pure take
refuge in us,
            to reign
⟨sit on throne⟩ in us,
survivors
— [or in

•

fut — et qui était
lié à lui, orga-
nisé — lequel
peut, pur se ré-
fugier en nous,
            régner
⟨trôner⟩ en nous,
survivants
— [ou en

〈3

absolute purity,
on which
time pivots and
is formed again —
   [once 〈in〉 God]
   was the most divine

———

•

〈3

la pureté absolue,
sur laquelle le
temps pivote et
se refait —
   [jadis 〈en〉 Dieu]
   état le plus divin

———

166

I who know it
for him   carry a
            terrible
            secret!
    father —
    he, too much
child for
such things

——————

    I know it, it is in
this that his being is
perpetuated —

    •

moi qui le sais
pour lui   porte un
            terrible
            secret!
    père —
    lui, trop
enfant pour
de telles choses

——————

    je le sais, c'est en
cela que son être est
perpétué —

I feel it in me
who wants — if not
the lost life,
at least the equi-
valent —

death
— or one is stripped
of a body
— in those who remain

•

je le sens en moi
qui veut — sinon
la vie perdue,
du moins l'équi-
valent —

la mort
— ou l'on est dépouillé
de corps
— en ceux qui restent

(I

168

and then III
   to speak to him in this way
      is it not that
Friend, ⟨say that⟩
you triumph
⟨is it⟩ is it not
detached from ⟨your⟩ all
⟨my⟩ weight of
life
— from the old
pain of living
      (oh! I

•

(I

et alors III
   lui parler ainsi
      n'est-ce pas que
Ami, ⟨dis que⟩
tu triomphes
⟨n'es⟩ n'est-ce pas
dégagé de ⟨ton⟩ tout
⟨ma⟩ poids de la
vie
— du vieux
mal de vivre
      (oh! je

⟨2

    feel you
so strongly — and that you
are always
well with
us, father, mother,
⟨meadows⟩ — but
free, eternal
child, and everywhere
at once —
_____

  and the underside
     — I can

•

⟨2

    bien fort
te sens — et que tu
te trouves bien
toujours avec
nous, père, mère,
⟨prés⟩ — mais
libre, enfant
éternel, et partout
à la fois —
_____

  et les dessous
    — je peux

170

say that because
I keep all my
pain for us —
— the pain of
not being — that
you do not know
— and that I
impose on myself
(cloistered, further-
more, outside of

•

dire cela parce que
je garde toute ma
douleur pour nous —
— la douleur de
ne pas être — que
tu ignores
— et que je
m'impose
(cloîtré, du
reste, hors de la

(4
life where you
lead me
        (having opened
for us a
world of death)
        ——

·

                    (4
vie où tu me
mènes
        (ayant ouvert
pour nous un
monde de mort)
        ——

(ɪ

172

moral
burial
——   father mother
Oh
   do not hide
him yet,
      etc. ——

friend earth awaits
—— the pious act, of
hiding him
         —— leaves

•

                              (ɪ
l'ensevelissement
moral
——   père mère
Oh
   ne le cache
pas encore,
      etc. ——

amie la terre attend
—— l'acte pieux, de
le cacher
         —— laisse

(2
the other mother —
common
to all men —
 [in which goes
the bed — where he is
now]
to take him
— leaves the
men who have come
— oh! the

·

(2
l'autre mère —
commune de
tous les hommes —
 [dans laquelle va
le lit — où il est
maintenant]
le prendre
— laisse les
hommes apparus
— oh! les

174

(3
men — these
men [under-
takers — or
friends?]
    to carry him away
followed by tears
    — etc —
towards earth
mother of all

•

(3
les hommes — ces
hommes [croque
morts — ou
amis?]
    l'emporter
suivi de larmes
    — etc —
vers terre
mère à tous

                    (4
mother of all — his
now
        and
(since she already
  partakes of you, your
  grave dug by
  him?)
        he
now become a face
        little man
        somber like a man
        _____

                ·

                        (4
    mère à tous — la
    sienne maintenant
            et
    (puisqu'elle participe
    déjà de toi, ta
    fosse creusée par
    lui?)
            lui
    devenu visage
        petit homme
        grave d'homme
        _____

176

accomplices
of death
it is

during
sickness
— I
thinking
mother — ?
and knowing

•

complices
de mort
c'est

pendant
maladie
— moi
pensant
mère — ?
et sachant

to close his eyes
— I do not want
to close his eyes —
    — that will look
    at me always

   ———

or death aside
  closed eyes, etc.
we see him again in sickness
struggling against this horrible
state —

                 ●

        fermer les yeux
      — je ne veux pas
        fermer les yeux —
             — qui me regar-
            deront toujours

      ———

     ou mort à part
       yeux fermés, etc.
     on le revoit en maladie
     luttant contre cet état
     gênant —

little body
put to the side
by death
a hand

that a moment
before was him

— and cry, almost without
paying attention to this
body put aside —
O my son
as toward a heaven
spiritual instinct

•

petit corps
mis de côté
par mort
une main

qui un instant
avant était lui

— et cri, sans presque
faire attention à ce
corps mis à part —
O mon fils
comme vers un ciel
instinct spiritualiste

suspense
— break —
part
—

Oh! this sacrifice —
for that to deny
his life
— to bury him
—

let us talk about him
again, let us extinguish
— in reality, silence

•

suspens
— rupture —
partie
—

Oh! ce sacrifice —
pour cela nier
sa vie
— pour l'ensevelir
—

causons de lui
encore, éteignons
— en réalité, silence

180

$(1$

break　in two

I write — him
　　(underground)
　　　　decomposition
mother sees —
　　　what she should
　　　　　not know
　──
　　then sickness he comes back
up until ⟨com⟩, all
purified! (by disease) and
asleep — so beautiful dead
— tomb but fiction
(we make him disappear —
so he will remain in

•

$(1$

rupture　en deux

j'écris — lui
　　(sous terre)
　　　　décomposition
mère voit —
　　　ce qu'elle devrait
　　　　　ignorer
　──
　　puis maladie il revient
jusqu'à ce que ⟨com⟩, tout
épuré! (par mal) et
couché — si beau mort
— que fiction tombeau
(on le fait disparaître —
pour qu'il reste en

us
     his <u>look</u>
         (conscience)
  — for a long time
  watched during
    sickness

    ———

    or then
      triumph
  after —
           3rd part
break between I and II
  and between ⟨II and IV⟩
      II and III
   everything connects again

        —

•

               (2
nous
    (son <u>regard</u>
         (conscience)
  — longtemps
  regardé pendant
    maladie

    ———

    ou alors
      triomphe
  après —
          3e partie
rupture entre I et II
  et entre ⟨II et IV⟩
      II et III
   tout se rattache

        —

182

not to know his
happiness
    when he is
there — ... found that
so natural
—————

    link
        to unconsciousness
           of death —

•

ne pas savoir son
bonheur
    quand il est
là — ... trouvé cela
si naturel
—————

    relier
        à inconscience
           de mort —

true mourning in
the apartment
— not cemetery —

furniture

•

vrai deuil en
l'appartement
— pas cimetière —

meubles

184

to find only
absence —
— in presence
of little clothes
— etc —
mother.

•

trouver absence
seule —
— en présence
de petits vêtements
— etc —
mère.

            little sailor —
        sailor suit
                what!
        — for enormous
                    crossing
        a wave will carry you
                    ascetic
            sea,
                ⟨+ +⟩

                        •

                    petit marin —
                costume marin
                    quoi!
                — pour grande
                            traversée
                une vague t'emporta
                            ascète
                    mer,
                        ⟨+ +⟩

186

fiction
 of absence
  maintained by mother
   —   apartment
⟨no⟩   "I do not know
      what they have
      done — ⟨I have not⟩ in
      the trouble and
      tears of that time
      —   I only

—————

but she followed to the cemetery.

•

fiction
 de l'absence
  gardée par mère
   —   appartement
⟨non⟩   «je ne sais pas
      ce qu'ils en ont
      fait — ⟨je n'ai⟩ dans
      le trouble et les
      pleurs d'alors
      —   je sais seule-

—————

mais elle a suivi au cimetière.

know that he is no longer
here

and if, he is there — absent —
from which mother herself
has become phantom —
spiritualized by
habit of living
with a vision

(2

•

ment qu'il n'est plus
ici

    et si, il y est — absent —
    d'où mère elle-même
    fantôme devenue —
    spiritualisée par
    habitude de vivre
    avec une vision

(2

188

(3

while he
father — who
was building the
tomb —
  will wall up .....
          knows
— and won't his spirit
go looking for
the traces of
                and trans-
    destruction —   mute into
                pure
                spirit?

·

                    (3
  tandis que lui
  père — qui
  construisit le
  tombeau —
    mura .....
              sait
    — et son esprit
  n'y va-t-il pas cher-
  cher les traces de
                  et trans-
      destruction —   muer en
                  esprit
                  pur?

with the result that
purity emerges from
corruption!

•

si bien que la
pureté sort de
la corruption!

no — I will not
give up
nothingness

———

father — — — I
feel nothingness
invade me

•

non — je ne
laisserai pas
le néant

———

père — — — je
sens le néant
m'envahir

and if at least
  — spirit —
I have not given
adequate blood —
    —
  that my thought
  make for him a
  purer more
      beautiful life.

  _____

— and like his fear of me — who
thinks — beside him —

•

          et si au moins
            — esprit —
          je n'ai pas donné
          sang suffisant —
              —
            que ma pensée
            lui fasse une
            vie plus belle
                plus pure.

            _____

          — et comme sa peur de moi — qui
          pense — à côté de lui —

192

What, the thing I am saying
is true — it is not
only
music ————
    etc.

•

Quoi, ce que je dis
est vrai — ce n'est
pas seulement
musique ————
    etc.

bouquets

we feel obliged
to throw into this earth
that opens in front
of the child — the most
beautiful bouquets —
the ⟨flowers⟩ most beautiful
products, of this
earth — sacrificed
— to veil

•

bouquets

on se sent obligé
de jeter en cette terre
qui s'ouvre devant
l'enfant — les plus
beaux bouquets —
les ⟨fleurs⟩ plus beaux
produits, de cette
terre — sacrifiés
— pour voiler

(2

194   (or pay for him
           what he owes —
           ———

•

                              (2
           (ou lui faire
           payer son forfait —
           ———

II

struggle
  of the two
  father and son
  the one
to preserve son in
thought — ideal —
the other to
live, rising up
again etc —
  — interruptions
    deficiency)

—

•

II

lutte
  des deux
  père et fils
l'un pour
conserver fils en
pensée — idéal —
l'autre pour
vivre, se relevant
etc —
  — interruptions
    carence)

—

(2

thus
and mother cares
for him well —
cares of mother
interrupting thought
— and child
between father who thinks
him dead, and mother
life —
———— "cares for him well
etc.
— from which

•

(2

ainsi
et mère soigne
le bien —
soins de mère
interrompant pensée
— et enfant
entre père qui le
pense mort, et mère
vie —
———— «soigne le bien
etc.
— d'où

It is only in III
that <u>burst</u> of this
(shattering) caused
by cry of I —
⟨and⟩ little by little
fits together —
all finished

•

⟨3

Ce n'est qu'en III
qu'<u>éclat</u> de ceci
(brisure) causé
par cri de I —
⟨et⟩ se raccorde
peu à peu —
tout fini

198

child
          (m
destiny
earth calls it
consoling
—

•

enfant
          (m
destinée
terre le dit
consolante
—

The grave father
  he belongs
    to me
not having given being
  to let it be
  lost
        — trouble
and mother — I do not want
  him to stop
      (idea there!)

•

Le père grave
    c'est à moi
      qu'il appartient
ayant donné l'être
  de ne pas le laisser
  perdre
        — trouble
  et mère — je ne veux
    pas qu'il cesse
      (idée là!)

appeared!
        — shadow   (1
        my mother
        mother and son
            up to +

from the wretched day
and which I do
not doubt

.

apparue!
        — ombre   (1
        ma mère
        mère et fils
            jusqu'au +

du jour pauvre
et dont je ne me
doutais pas

if it is not
            punishment
    the children of other
                    classes

    _____

so that
    furious
    against +
        vile society
        that had to
                crush him
                perhaps

•

                                    (2
si ce n'est
            chatiment
    les enfants des autres
                        classes

    _____

alors que
    furieuse
    contre +
        société vile
        qui devait
                    l'écraser
                    peut-être

202

by recovering from
    an illness
    for me to recapture
    that
        p.haps

·

par la guéri d'un
    mal
    me rattrappe
    à cela
        p. être

Design by David Bullen
Typeset in Mergenthaler Garamond #3
by Wilsted & Taylor
Printed by Maple-Vail
on acid-free paper

DATE DUE

WITHDRAWN